Published by Motivational Press, Inc., 7668 El Camino Real, #104-223, Carlsbad, CA 92009
Copyright © 2010 by Ruth Anderson.

ISBN: 978-0-9825755-6-7

Written by Ruth D. Anderson, Ph.D.
www.HairpinTurn.org

Publisher: Motivational Press, Inc
www.MotivationalPress.com

Dedication

To all women of all ages in all stages of life —
who always and everywhere
have the potential to change
everything

contents

"Stories are medicine. They have such power; they do not require that we do, be, act anything—we need only listen. The remedies for repair or reclamation of any lost psychic drive are contained in stories."

— C L A R I S S A   P I N K O K A   E S T E S

Introduction

This workbook accompanies the book *Hairpin Turn: Trusting Your Heart's Direction in Leadership and Life*. At the end of the chapters in *Hairpin Turn*, you are invited to participate in practices designed to help you make the shift towards another way to lead and, in fact, towards an alternative way to live. In this workbook, you will reflect further and explore other practices that can move you in the direction of your heart's intelligence.

You may want to work through this workbook alone, or you may find it helpful to work in a small group with others. In either case, give yourself some time to reflect on your life as it is now, and then give yourself permission to envision what life might be like when you trust the wisdom of your heart, stand in your body's wisdom, and think with a spacious mind.

The reflections and practices are suggestions intended to help you experience life from a place of authenticy, energy and grace. In order to do this, sometimes you will need to gently unravel the condition of your current life.

As you read the Ruthie stories sprinkled throughout *Hairpin Turn* and collected in *Ruthie Stories*, reflect back on the energy and the wisdom you left behind as a pre-adolescent girl. Recognize that she is within you, wanting to inform your life still.

Resolve Today

Resolve means to declare an intention with firmness, to vow, to decide and ultimately to move in a direction of change. In the world of music, resolve or resolution is the need for a sounded note or chord to move from a dissonance or an unstable sound to a consonance, a more final or stable-sounding one. "Resolve Today" offers a framework to help you make the shift from surviving to thriving in your daily life. This practice was introduced in *Hairpin Turn* and can be an added component to the exercises in this workbook.

At the beginning of each day, you will:
    Review your upcoming day in your mind
    Engage your intention for the upcoming day
During your day you will:
    See and sense your thoughts and actions, become an observer
    Occupy your life with heart, mind and body practices
    Love in ways that delight you and others
At the end of the day you will:
    Validate and value the life that you lived this day
    End your day with gratitude.
Continue to Resolve each day and use the practices in this workbook to supplement your choices that will support making the hairpin turn in your life.

Paradoxes

You will notice that in this workbook, you are invited to hold the tension of who you have been, who you are now and who you are becoming all at the same time. This is part of the journey. You are asked to look back and notice how the girl you left behind might inform your current life while, at the same time, you reflect on that which no longer serves you. Sometimes you are encouraged to add to your life (like incorporating a life-giving simplicity practice into your life); other times you are nudged to subtract (like dropping a commitment which you frankly dread). You will walk the edge of relinquishing parts of your ego and yet also establishing parts of yourself.

You have unique gifts to offer those around you and you have a special shadow side that gets you in trouble. When you realize that you hold both darkness and light within you, then you open up to a world of compassion for yourself and for others. Your "outside life" changes to the degree to which you change your "inside life." This is the foundation for making the hairpin turn.

"If we are to live our lives fully and well, we must learn to embrace the opposites, to live in a creative tension between our limits and our potentials. We must honor our limitation in ways that do not distort our nature and we must trust and use our gifts in ways that fulfill the potentials God gave us."
— P A R K E R   P A L M E R

A Word about Flow Writing

At a "Self as Source" workshop, Christina Baldwin teaches us about a way to write called free flow writing. Before this, I had written for academe and business but that writing did not have this kind of energy and creativity. It is simple and is the single process that transformed my relationship with my writing and with myself. You might want to use this process for prompts within each section. I have given you plenty of space to write about your "true self" in this workbook.

Here are the simple "rules" of the "flow writing" process:

1. Keep your pen moving and write without interruption for 5-10 minutes. No matter what, keep writing. Use the space provided in this workbook—or have extra paper or a journal available.
2. Be specific. Instead of "flower" write "daisy."
3. Lose control (very important). Set aside any fear and stick with the raw idea. Allow the story to write itself.
4. Do not worry about spelling or punctuation.
5. Feel free to be mushy or crude—anything goes!

This writing process helped me "let go" and lean into trusting the deepest wisdom that was hidden way down inside my crusty adult self.

My hope for you is that these prompts stir up in you the wisdom that is already within you—and waiting for you still.

Trust the Energy of Your Heart

Above all, trust the good, warm energy of your heart's intelligence as you move through this workbook. With your body grounded and strong, your mind clear and curious, and your heart open and flowing with compassion, you will make the hairpin turn with both stillness and glee.

Groups

If you decide to do this work with others, consider using the principles and practices of Circle as outlined by Christina Baldwin, www.peerspirit.com

THREE PRINCIPLES:
- Leadership rotates among members of group
- Responsibility is shared
- Center is held by reliance on Spirit

THREE PRACTICES:
attentive listening
intentional speaking
contribute to group's well being

FOUR AGREEMENTS:
What is shared in the circle remains in the circle;
We listen to each other with compassion and curiosity;
Each person asks for what she or he needs and offers what she or he can;
Whenever uncertain or in need of a resting point, we agree to fall into silence, and wait for guidance.

A Celtic Blessing for You

May the light of your soul guide you.

May the light of your soul bless the work that you do with the secret love and warmth of your heart.

May you see in what you do the beauty of your own soul.

May the sacredness of your work bring healing, light and renewal to those who work with you and to those who see and receive your work.

May your work never weary you.

May it release within you wellsprings of refreshment, inspiration and excitement.

May you be present in what you do.

May you never become lost in bland absences.

May the day never burden.

May dawn find you awake and alert, approaching your new day with dreams, possibilities and promises.

May evening find you gracious and fulfilled.

May you go into the night blessed, sheltered and protected.

May your soul calm, console and renew you.

"How we remember, what we remember, and why we remember form the most personal map of our individuality."

— C H R I S T I N A   B A L D W I N

The Leader Within

"Few are those who see with their own eyes and feel with their own hearts."

— ALBERT EINSTEIN

W e all need meaning in our lives. We feel alive and engaged when we unleash our potential into the world in which we live. From early childhood, we hold a sense of wonder about the possible purpose for our lives. Well-meaning adults bend down and ask us: "What do you want to be when you grow up?" and we respond with some dreams borrowed from television or books or the adults we see each day. We may say "Tinkerbell" or "teacher" or "a mom." Many adults, past mid-life, half-heartedly laugh and confess: "I am still trying to find out what I am going to do when I grow up." Throughout our lives, we hold onto a sense that our being here on earth matters.

All of us sense that we have the capacity to be leaders, yet often we are not quite sure what this might mean in our lives. We have had hints of inspired leadership when very young or glimpses of an authentic purpose at various points in our lives. However, many of us have been discouraged from pursuing our life's purpose and may even have concluded that living a life of meaning will "just have to wait" until maybe retirement—if ever.

Getting Started

This workbook, designed to help you unleash the leader within you, asks you to respond to the prompts with the enthusiasm and creativity of the child you left behind. Allow yourself to explore and dream and bring voice to that which is already within you.

"I know now that anything one can do on behalf of true self is done ultimately in the service of others."

— PARKER PALMER

The Leader Within You: Expressed

Tell a story about a time—as a child—when you were a leader. Perhaps you were chosen to be "Safety" at school or you were a babysitter for a neighbor. Describe what happened:

Describe how this leadership role made you feel—what changed for you?

Q What did you learn about yourself as a leader in this role?

Q What was the gift of this childhood leadership experience?

"If I had influence with the good fairy who is supposed to preside over the

christening of all children, I should ask that her gift to each child in the world be

a sense of wonder so indestructible that it would last throughout life."

— R A C H E L   C A R S O N

The Leader Within You: Depressed

Q Tell another story about a time—as a child—when your leadership potential was squashed. Perhaps a teacher told you that you could not sing (and you knew otherwise) or that your good ideas were not needed. What happened?

D Describe how this made you feel—what changed for you?

What did you learn about yourself as a leader from this experience?

"Authentic leaders in every setting—from families to nation-states—aim at liberating the heart, their own and others', so that its powers can liberate the world."

— Parker Palmer

Making the Hairpin Turn

Allow yourself to "re-experience" this past through explaining to your younger self how this is just not true. Provide details so that your younger self can unravel this mis-perception. You may start by saying something like: "Ruthie, these adults were doing their best but they did not have any idea how smart you were in math. Remember how you collected money during the talent shows in the neighborhood."

Reinvented Leader

In *Hairpin Turn*, the reinvented leader engages the whole self in everyday life. This leader leaves old paradigms of leading and living behind and embraces a leadership of grace, focused energy and trust in all of life's experiences. With the heart awakened, the mind open, and the body grounded, a leader engages at her full capacity. Part of the challenge for us involves giving up old notions of leadership as an exclusive activity only available for a finite number of people who "head" organizations. Let's play around with shifting our basic ideas about who is a leader.

Old Ideas about Leaders and Leadership

List the leaders in your community when you were growing up and what made them leaders (for example: the town mayor—he had power to fix potholes in our community):

"It sounds impossible, even ridiculous to say that compassion and peace

can be accomplished in our world through each of us working on the conditions of our

hearts and minds, but there seems to be no other way."
— GERALD MAY

New Ideas about Leaders and Leadership

List who you knew when you were young who might not have been labeled by others as a leader, but you knew had power (like the lady next door who arranged to take food to neighbors who were sick):

You as Reinvented Leader

List the ways you are a leader in your everyday life (as a grandmother; as a PTA member on a committee; as a neighbor; as a team member; as the person who hires and interacts with babysitters):

"Real Power is always an exchange of power. It is always the deep purpose

of leadership to use power to call out the God-given power of others."
— BENNETT SIMS

Your Power, Redefined

One of the most important realizations on the journey towards a new way to lead, and a new way to be, involves how we view power and where we "get" authority in our lives. In the previous brainstorming, notice that the traditional view of leadership suggests that power is assigned to some people and not to others. For example, the mayor has been given power as has the principal of the school or the executive director of a nonprofit. This is a limited view of leadership. Real leadership comes from the authority and power we have inside us—always available to bring into the present moment.

This power, full of faith in our own special giftedness, arises from a deep truth we know lies within us—yet it is frequently hidden. An essential part of this journey is to reclaim the power we have within us and then to trust this internal authority in all we think, do and say.

Practices for Taking a New Direction Your Life

Daily Power Surges

Reflect on the past 24 hours in your life. List the moments you felt most alive or when you felt you were most able to give and receive from a stance of full capacity:

Power Outages

Now reflect on the past 24 hours in your life but consider the moments you felt most drained or when you were least able to give and receive from full capacity:

Checklist for the Hairpin Turn in My Life

_____ Leave behind the "depressed" childhood definitions of myself

_____ Re-discover the "expressed" childhood definitions of myself

_____ Let go of traditional definitions of leadership

_____ Embrace the new leadership within me

_____ Release old notions of power and authority

_____ Affirm the power with me

_____ Notice, each 24 hours, my power surges and power outages

Insights for the Journey

"Dwell in possibility."
— EMILY DICKINSON

Trusting the Intelligence of Your Heart

"When you begin to touch your heart or let your heart be touched, you begin to discover that it's bottomless, that it doesn't have any resolution, that this heart is huge, vast, and limitless. You begin to discover how much warmth and gentleness is there, as well as how much space."

— PEMA CHODRON

Nothing is more crucial for taking a new direction in life than you understanding how the quality of your heart's energy impacts every aspect of your existence. When you meet life with an open and engaged heart, you are an amazing human being. You are creative, joyful and interested in everything that is happening in the present moment. When you meet life with a closed heart, you are wary of others, you spend time crafting your self-image and you hold onto moods that are destructive to you and others around you. In our culture, we are taught that the mind can be cultivated to somehow bring us happiness and peace and intelligence. Actually, only the heart's intelligence can offer the kind of life we are seeking.

The Leader Within You:
Expressed Through Trusting Your Heart

Describe a time in your life as a child when your heart was open, soft, present and awake. You may want to check out some Ruthie stories from Hairpin Turn to remind yourself of when your heart "just knew" what to say or do in a specific situation:

Describe the authenticity and the innocence and the aliveness in that childhood condition—when your heart's intelligence was expressed:

Now describe a specific situation in your current adult life when your heart was fully expressed—and you felt much like this child you left behind:

"Spiritual love is a position of standing with one hand extended into the universe and one hand extended into the world, letting ourselves be a conduit for passing energy."
— CHRISTINA BALDWIN

The Leader Within You:
Depressed By Not Trusting Your Heart

Outline a time recently in which you were concerned about your prestige and what you did to "adapt" to affect others (for example, you may have slipped into the conversation your MBA degree, the upgrades in your kitchen renovation, or that you were nominated for an award):

What might be a recent example when you held onto a mood or resentment and, in some way, stayed stuck in the past and therefore were not able to engage in the present?

"We must take a conscious journey into the dynamics of our emotional undercurrents to see patterns and to break the patterns."
— MICHAEL BROWN

Making the Hairpin Turn

Recalculate what your life might "look like" if, instead of the concern about your prestige with your adaptations to please others, you shifted to a life of authenticity, truthfulness and forgiveness. What might the child you left behind teach the older, more guarded self? See if you can write out what the one might say to the other—for the fun of it!

"There is something in every one of you that waits and listens for the sound of the genuine in yourself. It is the only true guide you will ever have.
And if you cannot hear it, you will all of your life spend your
days on the ends of strings that somebody else pulls."
— HAROLD THURMAN

Practices for Taking a New Direction in Your Life: Towards Trusting Your Heart

Become Aware of the Messengers in Your Life
In your daily life, begin to notice when you react negatively to people or circumstances. Simply become aware of your emotional reaction with a self-statement like, "well, isn't that interesting," and then notice how much you want to blame them for your emotional state. Simply notice your reaction and name it "interesting" and see if you can shift your automatic, blaming reaction to more of a conscious response of your choosing over time.

Observe any patterns in your reactions (hint: these people live with you and work with you) and see if you can, with a light heart, keep from "shooting the messenger." Name a few individuals who you know "push your bottons" and see if you can start your new practice with them:

Shift to Your Compassionate Heart

During the day, gently shift your focus from thinking, analyzing and strategizing to the emotional quality of energy surrounding your heart. You might even say to yourself: "Shift to my heart" and touch your chest area as a cue to let go of thoughts and shift to your heart's intelligence. Allow yourself to settle into a relaxed awareness of the compassion always available in your heart. You might want to take a few minutes during some part of the routine of your day to shift to your compassionate heart.

List a few times during your day when you might remind yourself that your heart's compassion is available to inform your life (for example, when you shower in the morning, on your drive to work, as you drive into the driveway at night, before retiring at night):

"In moments of doubt, I find it best to surrender myself to trust."
— ROSEMARY DOUGHERTY

Checklist for Taking the Hairpin Turn in My Life

_____ Daily notice when and with whom my heart is open, soft, present and awake

_____ Don't shoot the messenger—just observe with "interesting"

_____ Let go of adapting to affect others

_____ Embrace truthfulness in all areas of my life

_____ Shift consciously several times a day to the compassion present in my heart

_____ Identify and unleash the emotional authenticity of the child I left behind

Insights for the Journey

Opening Your Mind

"The true sign of intelligence is not knowledge but imagination."
— ALBERT EINSTEIN

Recognizing that your mind can be your best friend or your worst enemy gives you power and moves you in the direction towards freedom in your life. Your mind can drive you crazy, and it also has the potential to provide extraordinary capacity for inner guidance.

The Leader Within You:
Expressed Through Opening Your Mind

Tell a story about a time, as a child or as a young adult, when your peaceful, quiet mind opened to what was happening in the moment. Describe a situation in which you "just knew" what needed to happen next (sometimes this happens in the middle of a chaotic situation and other times you "just felt supported" to do or say something—although you could not explain how you knew):

Describe how your quiet mind felt in this situation.

What was the gift of this opening of your mind experience?

"The brain is wider than the sky."
— EMILY DICKINSON

The Leader Within You: Depressed
Through Mental Chatter

Tell another story about a recent time when your thinking just about drove you crazy. You were filled with strategies, doubt, anxiety and fear:

Describe how this mental chatter made you feel. What was the outcome?

"Only when we are no longer afraid do we begin to live."
— DOROTHY THOMPSON

Making the Hairpin Turn

Allow yourself to "re-experience" this recent experience and shift it from mental chatter to quiet mind by having your younger self coach your more current self on how to open the mind:

Reinvented Leader

Bring to mind a situation in your current life that challenges you and one you have spent some time attempting to clarify. (You will use this situation in the next practice):

Practices for Taking a New Direction in Your Life: Opening Your Mind

Thinking with Your Heart

Bring to mind the previous situation and then deliberately let it drop into the space around your heart. You may want to touch your chest area in order to locate the idea as resting in your heart. Then allow your thinking to shift gently into considering all the ways you appreciate this situation. Stay focused on feeling compassion, below your thinking center, and examine this situation as good news.

With your heart full of compassion, ask the question: How might this challenging situation actually be the answer to the dilemma I have been considering?:

> *"The major block to compassion is the judgment in our minds.*
> *Judgment is the mind's primary tool of separation."*
> — DIANE BERKE

Sitting in Silence

Make time during the day to pause and clear your mind. Refresh the screen of your mind in order to get updated information.

Name some times during your day when you can take between one and three minutes to pause, move below thinking, and refresh your thinking:

> *"We could never learn to be brave and patient*
> *if there were only joy in the world."*
> — HELEN KELLER

Checklist for the Hairpin Turn in My Life

____ Rediscover the feeling of my quiet mind

____ Let go of my mental chatter and fear of the future

____ Re-establish my thinking from a heart full of compassion

____ Release patterns of thoughts that do not serve me or others

____ Affirm the power of the spacious, calm mind

____ Practice meditating which quiets my busy mind

Insights for the Journey

*"I like living. I have sometimes been wildly, despairingly, acutely miserable,
racked with sorrow, but through it all
I still know quite certainly that just to be alive is a grand thing."*
— A G A T H A   C H R I S T I E

Moving Your Body

"Our bodies will speak to us, tell us what they don't want, what they can't handle anymore. Our bodies will tell us what hurts, what we are allergic to, what we wish to move away from."

— M E L O D Y   B E A T T I E

The body is the platform that holds the thinking heart and the spacious mind. A strong and relaxed body provides the strength and courage to think with your heart and to open to new understandings with a spacious mind. Without a grounded body, the mind flits around and the heart becomes cloudy with self-doubt. A relaxed yet alert body allows you to access your full intellectual capacity.

The Leader Within You:
Expressed Through a Relaxed, Grounded Body

Tell a story about a time, as a child, when your body was somehow connected to all of life — when you were relaxed and your senses were fully engaged:

*"Don't ask what the world needs. Ask what makes you come alive, and go do it.
Because what the world needs is people who have come alive."*
— HAROLD THURMAN

The Leader Within You:
Depressed Through a Tense and Irritated Body

Tell another story about a recent time when your body was tense or numb to what was happening around you:

"Once we accept our limits, we go beyond them."
— ALBERT EINSTEIN

Making the Hairpin Turn

Allow yourself to "re-experience" this past through the senses of the child you left behind. How might you "re-do" this recent experience with a sense of inner strength and grounded awareness from your physical presence:

"People are like stained glass windows: they sparkle and shine when the sun is out, but when the darkness sets in their true beauty is revealed only if there is a light within."

— ELIZABETH KUBLER-ROSS

Reinvented Leader

We treat our bodies as if they are machines separated from the rest of our lives. We have been taught to "be tough" and to "push through" pain or stress in order to get to some imaginary "other side." In fact, many of us become addicted to the rush and push of our accelerated pace—until the frenzied pace makes our bodies sick. This is one way our bodies get a rest! In order to become the fully expressed person we are seeking, we must shift from a frenzied pace to a friendly pace. We must become aware that our bodies hold a tremendous capacity when healthy and vibrant but can become a barrier to the potential within us when pushed beyond normal limits.

When healthy, our bodies provide us with "gut" or instinctive knowledge that guides us in all we think, say and do. Reinvented leaders take their bodies very seriously and know that the body is the platform for all other programs in their lives.

List What You Already Know

Write out what you know about how eating, sleeping, exercising and drinking water impacts your body and then consider what actions you take in each area:

"If we do not transform the pain in our lives, we transmit it."
— RICHARD ROHR

Practices for Taking a New Direction in Your Life: Moving Your Body

Befriending Our Reactivity

This practice interrupts your reactivity, which often leads to a forceful or automatic response. This practice pauses you and invites you to more readily come into the current moment—as experienced in your body through your reaction. This practice helps to become grounded in your body wisdom through encouraging you to actually "befriend our reactivity."

Steps for Befriending Reactivity:

Notice Your Reaction
When you notice you are reacting to some situation or person, pause and become grounded and receptive to "release" from your normal automatic response.

Accept Your Reaction
Befriend your reactivity in a non-judgmental way.

Pause
Stop your automatic response by asking: What is beneath the reactivity?

Befriend
Daily say: "May I embrace my reactivity today as a means of experiencing my aliveness."

From your previous example above (the situation in which your body went numb or tense), describe how you might have befriended reactivity, using the steps described above:

"No reward anyone might give us could possibly be greater than the reward that comes from living by our own best lights."
— PARKER PALMER

Checklist for the Hairpin Turn in My Life

__ Recognize when my body is both relaxed and alert

__ Understand that the vitality in my body is linked with all my other capacities

__ Let go of pushing my limits physically

__ Befriend my reactivity

__ Practice basic self-care in my eating, drinking, exercising and sleeping

Insights for the Journey

"Your center is a place you can trust. It connects your body, mind, heart, and soul.
It connects truth, your inner voice and the Divine. Your best work comes from there."
— MELODY BEATTIE

Becoming Yourself

"The beginning is always today."

— MARY WOLLSTONECRAFT

Even though we hate to admit it, most of us recognize that we have "gone far away" from our true selves. As we have grown into adulthood, we have unconsciously allowed our culture to influence how we define ourselves. Instead of accepting our unique gifts and personality, we seem to resist that which comes naturally to us. We end up pretending to be someone else instead. This combination of acting out of a false self and also of resentment for what we do not have or cannot do very well creates tremendous stress in our lives. Investigating ourselves and moving in the direction of both self-acceptance and also self-development allows us to make the hairpin turn that we are seeking with grace.

The Leader Within You: Expressed By Being Yourself

Tell a story about a time, as a child or teenager, when you felt totally yourself — when your "funny" way of being was actually appreciated and loved:

Describe your personality in terms of basic preferences in any way that makes sense to you — "I am a quiet person who loves to read; I am an extrovert who enjoys nature." (You may want to go to www.EnneagramInstitute.com to take a free personality assessment to explore your personality further.):

"Whoever said anybody has a right to give up?"
— MARIAN WRIGHT EDELMAN

The Leader Within You: Depressed By Not Being Yourself

Tell another story about a recent time when you felt "pushed" out of your personality-comfort zone in ways that were truly distressing:

Making the Hairpin Turn

Allow yourself to "re-experience" this past experience through exploring what your "true self" might say to your "false self" to encourage you to lean into your truest (and best) identity:

"And as we let our own light shine, we unconsciously give other people permission to do the same. As we are liberated from our fear, our presence automatically liberates others."
— MARIANNE WILLIAMSON

Reinvented Leader

The reinvented leader has fun acknowledging who she is and who she is not. She readily knows her personality preferences and she knows what happens to her personality when stressed. She confesses her humanity to others and by her own authenticity she supports others in being their own best selves. She exhibits massive self-understanding and compassion.

The invitation available to you is to simply and radically become yourself — which makes room for others to be their best true selves as well. This allows you to lean into your own authentic energy, let go of all the effort it takes in pretending to be someone else, and opens up a way to focus your energy to become the person you are meant to be.

"There are years that ask questions and years that answer."
— ZORA HURSTON

Practices for Taking a New Direction in Your Life: Becoming Yourself

Inner Smile

This practice is a simple way of making an inward shift of perspective and connecting with the positive energy of self-compassion. Whenever you feel stuck in the energy of negativity, try this for a moment: Close your eyes. Get in touch with yourself, get in touch with your inner self, your inner being, that part of yourself that is most deeply you, and allow your inner being to smile. Not the "smile for others to see," but a smile that begins behind your eyes — deep down and in — and is directed first toward yourself and your life, a smile that says "yes" to life. In spite of all the challenges, yes. That smile is like a comforting hand, a warm blanket, a long-lost friend… a blessing. Receive the blessing.

Allow your entire being, every cell in your body, to receive the positive, life-giving energy of this blessing – which flows from a simple "inner smile." Take a few minutes and give yourself an inner smile and write about your experience:

Checklist for the Hairpin Turn in My Life

_____ Lean into radical self-acceptance

_____ Notice and give up pretending to be other than who I am

_____ Practice self-compassion each day

_____ Smile inwardly to myself frequently throughout the day

_____ Discover something about my personality—through such assessments as the Enneagram
www.EnneagramInstitute.com

Insights for the Journey

"Above all be patient with the slow work of God."
— TEILLARD DE CHARDIN

Organized Focus

"The world needs dreamers and the world needs doers.
But above all, the world needs dreamers who do."
— SARAH BAN BREATHNACH

A s you become more aware of your personality, or your unique way of being in the world, you will notice that you come alive when you engage in certain activity and are drained when doing other activities. In other words, you are noticing both your special way of being (through personality assessment and knowledge) and your unique way of doing (through an inventory of skills). You are getting in touch with your unique capacities—which ultimately translates into organizing your focus into a certain work during each stage of your life. With humility, you receive as good news that which you can do really well and essentially let go of those activites which are not "of your making."

Again, for reasons too complicated to enumerate here, you can spend a tremendous amount of energy resisting that which comes naturally to you and move in a direction which is both effortful and even damaging to you. The exploration and embrace of the work or activity that "lights you up" has the ability to change everything. You can access many free on-line assessments about the types of activity suited to your life through the Web site www.jobhuntersbible.com. These assessments help you understand your giftedness and also can help you move towards a more purposeful, focused life.

"Vocation at its deepest level is: This is something I can't not do, for reasons
I'm unable to explain to anyone else and don't
fully understand myself but that are nonetheless compelling."
— PARKER PALMER

The Leader Within You:
Expressed Through Organized Focus

Tell a story about a time, as a child or young adult, when you did something you were proud of and the "doing of it" seemed effortless and natural to you (organized a talent show for the neighborhood; took care of your pets; organized your family summer trip):

Describe any skills you used and how doing this made you feel.

"You need only claim the events of your life to make yourself yours.
When you truly possess all you have been and done. . .
you are fierce with reality."
— FLORIDA SCOTT MAXWELL

The Leader Within You:
Depressed Through Unorganized Focus

Tell another story about a recent time in which you were engaged in an activity that was "way beyond" your skill or comfort level—when you were doing something that you knew was not—and will never be—an activity you enjoy or have any natural inclination towards:

_____

_____

Describe in any greater detail the skills you tried to use and then how this made you feel.

"One of the reasons we have difficulty identifying our gifts
is that we have had no one to listen to us or even look at us."
— E L I Z A B E T H   O ' C O N N O R

Making the Hairpin Turn

Allow yourself to "re-experience" this recent experience through having an honest talk with yourself about these two situations. Let your capable self talk to your incompetent self in a kind way about finding more opportunities to express that which you do well and letting go (when possible) of those situations that frankly do not suit you:

"We resist the very idea of limits, regarding limits of all sorts as temporary and regrettable impositions on our lives. . . . We refuse to take no for an answer."
— PARKER PALMER

Reinvented Leader

All of us need to give up on being good at everything and instead lean into those skills and activities that we do with effortless grace. This gives us reason to combine our best efforts with the best efforts in others. In other words, moving in the direction of our own giftedness allows others to move into theirs. This produces a collaborative world seeking to affirm the magnificent talents among and between us.

When you can confess both your strengths and your weaknesses, you invite others around you to ask you to do what you are capable of doing and, likewise, you allow others the room to contribute from their ability. Good families and good teams recognize how desperately we need the different capacities within ourselves and those around us.

Describe a time you contributed both by confessing your limits and by asserting your potential:

"Despite the American myth, I cannot be or do whatever I desire—a truism, to be sure, but a truism we often defy. . . . there are some roles and relationships in which we thrive and others in which we wither and die."

— P A R K E R   P A L M E R

Practices for Taking a New Direction in Your Life: Organized Focus

Weekly Power Surges

Reflect on the past week in your life. List the moments when you were most engaged. What specifically were you doing (little activities count such as "cleaning the closet out" and "walking the dog" or "talking on the phone with a new friend"):

Weekly Power Outages

Now reflect on the past week in your life but consider the moments you felt most drained by an activity or when you were least able to give and receive from full capacity:

> *"The gifts of life are given by a generous God.*
> *It's a wonder, it's a miracle, it's an embarrassment, it's irrational,*
> *but God's abundance transcends the market economy."*
> — WALTER BRUEGGEMAN

How to Open Yourself to Your Life's Purpose with Three Questions

1. What is your inner voice saying to you? Listen to your inner voice. It takes practice to hear your true desires. Your passion will often come as a whisper or serendipitous event that reminds you of what is important and what makes you happy. What whispers have you heard in these past weeks?

2. Are you willing to take action? Step out. The friendly universe is waiting for you to move in the direction of your inner voice. Who might be someone you can talk with about your sense of direction in life? What action might you take to move in that direction (take a class, get a coach, begin a new practice, change a friendship):

3. What has some "juice" for you? Dwell in possibilities. Your energy could lead you in a lot of different directions to find fulfillment. Explore your life and unearth the things that bring you heart-felt joy. Here are some questions which might be of service:

- What interest or desire are you most afraid of admitting to yourself and others?
- Who might you know that is doing something you might like to do? Describe yourself doing it.
- How could you make the world a better place for yourself and others?
- What's stopping you from moving forward with investigating your call?

"Normal is getting dressed in clothes that you buy for work, driving through traffic in a car you are still paying for, in order to get to the job that you need so you can pay for the clothes, car, and house that you leave empty all day in order to live in it!"
— ELLEN GOODMAN

Checklist for the Hairpin Turn in My Life

__ Leave behind those "life-draining" activities

__ Explore the skills that are naturally mine

__ Affirm the natural abilities in those around me

__ Let go of effortfully trying to do it all

__ Notice when a skill seems easy and natural for me to do

__ Discover what I am good at through taking some assessments

Insights for the Journey

"Only a life lived for others is a life worthwhile."
— ALBERT EINSTEIN

Yield to the Present Moment

"There are two ways to live: you can live as if nothing is a miracle;
you can live as if everything is a miracle."

— ALBERT EINSTEIN

With your three centers aligned, you naturally connect with your true self. You delight in your strengths. You smile at your areas of non-strength. Because of your willingness to be self-compassionate, you communicate authentic concern for others. With this essence of your self firmly in place, you organize your life around that which calls you at your current stage in life. Uncluttered with ambiguity, you bring an energized focus to each task and relationship. With this awareness, you freely and fully experience each moment in a delicious way.

The Leader Within You:
Expressed Through Yielding to the Present Moment

Tell a story about a time when, as a child, you were wide open to what was happening in the present moment—your heart was alive with compassionate understanding, your mind was spacious and clear and your body was pulsating with strength:

D Describe how being in this state of aliveness made you feel:

"All serious daring starts from within."
— H A R R I E T T E   B E E C H E R   S T O W E

The Leader Within You:
Depressed Through Living in the Past or in the Future

D Tell another story about a time in your life in which you lived either in the past or in the future—but clearly not in the present moment. What was going on?:

Describe how this made you feel:

> "We can't take any credits for our talents.
> It's how we use them that counts."
> — MADELEINE L'ENGLE

Making the Hairpin Turn

Allow yourself to "re-experience" this past situation through giving voice to what this might have looked like if you had been living in the present moment:

> "It is not the magnitude of our actions
> but the amount of love that is put into them that matters."
> — MOTHER THERESA

"Simplicity of living, if deliberately chosen, implies a compassionate approach to life. It means that we are choosing to live our daily lives with some degree of conscious appreciation of the condition of the rest of the world."
— DUANE ELGIN

Reinvented Leader

As a reinvented leader in the making, you understand that one of the secrets to a fully expressed life is learning to love who you are and to adore the life you have been given. Instead of yearning for a different future or regretting a distant past, you breathe and stand fully and squarely in the present moment and know that "life is good."

Practices for Taking a New Direction in Your Life: Yielding to Now

Simply list what you genuinely appreciate about the life you are living right now:

"Silence of the heart is necessary so you can hear God everywhere — in the closing of the door, in the person who needs you, in the birds that sing, in the flowers, in the animals."
— MOTHER TERESA

Five Ways to Move into Simplicity— A Portal to the Present Moment

Make a short list of the four to five most important things in your life. What do you value most? What four to five things do you most want to do in your life? Notice if how you actually live your life matches what you list as most important. Simplifying and living in the aliveness of the present moment starts with knowing your priorities:

Drop one commitment.

Think about all the things in your life that you are committed to doing, and try to find one that you dread doing. Find something that does not give you much value but takes up your time (perhaps you're on a board or committee). Take action today and drop that commitment. Call someone, send an e-mail, and tell the appropriate person that you just do not have the time. You will feel relief. This will create more space for you to put energy into your stated priorities.

Purge a drawer.

Select one small area such as a drawer, half of your closet or the top of the dresser or the corner of the laundry room that you would like for your focus. Here's how to purge: 1) empty everything from the drawer or corner and put it into a pile. 2) From this pile, pick out only the items that are of value to you—which are those you use and love. 3) Get rid of the rest. Trash it or put it in your car to give away to someone who might need it. 4) Put the stuff you love and use back, in a neat and orderly manner.

Simplify your to-do list.

Take a look at your to-do list. If it's more than 8 to 10 items long, pare it down. Try to find at least a few items that can be eliminated, delegated, automated, outsourced, or ignored. Shorten the list as much as possible. This is a good habit to do once a week. Rushing through a long to-do list prevents you from being in the moment.

Single-task.

Instead of multi-tasking, give yourself the gift of doing one thing at a time. Remove all distractions. Stick to that one task until you have finished it. This one act alone will make a huge difference in both your stress level and your productivity. This will also increase your ability to notice and to yield to the present moment.

Notes to myself on what actions I will take from this list of five ways to simplify my life:

Checklist for the Hairpin Turn in My Life

___ Slow down each day and appreciate the life I have been given

___ Pay attention to when I am in the past or the future and "come on back"

___ Simplify my life as much as possible

___ Learn to pause and check in with my senses to become present

___ Ask: Is my mind clear? My heart awake? My body grounded?

___ Live according to my top priorities each day

Insights for the Journey

"I loaf and I invite my soul."
— WALT WHITMAN

After the Turn

"A dream is the bearer of a new possibility,
the enlarged horizon, the great hope."
— H A R O L D   T H U R M A N

"Learn from yesterday, live for today, hope for tomorrow. The important
thing is not to stop questioning."
— A L B E R T   E I N S T E I N

"The things we fear most in organizations — fluctuations, disturbances,
imbalances — are the primary sources of creativity."
— M A R G A R E T   W H E A T L E Y

"The world needs people with the patience and the passion to make
that pilgrimage not only for their own sake but also as a social and
political act. The world still waits for the truth that will set us free—
my truth, your truth, our truth—the truth that was seeded in the earth
when each of us arrived here formed in the image of God. Cultivating
that truth, I believe, is the authentic vocation of every human being."
— P A R K E R   P A L M E R

"Meaning is found in discovering our place of service to the whole."

— D A V I D   K O R T E N

The Leader Within You: Expressed

Envision your new life after your hairpin turn. Allow yourself to dream of what your daily life might look like if you lived with a trusting heart, an open mind, a healthy, grounded body. Describe what you could be doing if you were completely yourself as you organized your days around that which you did well. Detail what your life would be like if you lived with an aliveness and awareness in each moment of each day.

Create Your Own Unique Checklist
For the Hairpin Turn in Your Life:

✓

✓

✓

✓

✓

✓

✓